Joseph
the dreamer

Story by Penny Frank

Illustrated by Tony Morris

THE LION
STORY BIBLE

7

TRING · BELLEVILLE · SYDNEY

The Bible tells us
how God chose the Israelites to be his
special people. He made them a
promise that he would always love
and care for them. But they must
obey him.
Joseph was a young man whom
God used in a special way. You can
find the story of Joseph in your Bible
in Genesis from chapter 37 to the end.

Copyright © 1984 Lion Publishing

Published by
Lion Publishing plc
Icknield Way, Tring, Herts, England
ISBN 0 85648 732 5
Lion Publishing Corporation
10885 Textile Road, Belleville,
Michigan 48111, USA
ISBN 0 85648 732 5
Albatross Books
PO Box 320, Sutherland, NSW 2232, Australia
ISBN 0 86760 516 2

First edition 1984

Printed and bound in Hong Kong
by Mandarin Offset International (HK) Ltd.

**British Library Cataloguing in
Publication Data**
Frank, Penny
Joseph the dreamer. – (The Lion
Story Bible; 7)
1. Joseph (Biblical
patriarch) – Juvenile literature
I. Title   II. Morris, Tony
222'.110924   BS580.J6

ISBN 0-85648-732-5

**Library of Congress Cataloging in
Publication Data**
1. Joseph (Son of Jacob)—Juvenile
literature. 2. Bible. O.T.—Biography—
Juvenile literature. [1. Joseph (Son of
Jacob) 2. Bible stories—O.T.] I. Morris,
Tony, ill. II. Title. III. Series: Frank,
Penny. Lion Story Bible; 7.
BS580.J6F73 1984   222'.110924 [B]
84-17112
ISBN 0-85648-732-5

There was an old man called Jacob
living in Canaan. His wife had died,
but he was never lonely because he had
twelve sons.

Jacob loved all his sons, but one
was special. His name was Joseph.
And Jacob loved him best of all.

The other brothers were jealous
because Jacob made a big fuss over
Joseph. He even gave Joseph a special
coat to wear.

When Joseph told his brothers about the dream, they were really angry.

'Do you think we will bow down to you?' they said. 'You must be joking!'

Another time, Joseph dreamed he was
looking up into the sky. His family
were the sun, the moon and the stars.
They all bowed down to him.

Even his father was upset when he
heard about that dream.

'What kind of dream is that?' he said.
'Be quiet!'

His brothers hated him still more.

Jacob was a rich man. He had huge
flocks of sheep and goats.

The animals needed grass to eat and
water to drink. Often they had to be
taken a long way away to find the
grass and water.

Jacob's sons went with the animals to take care of them. Sometimes they walked many days just looking for grass.

Joseph stayed at home.

One day Jacob's sons had been away
with the sheep for a long time. Jacob
said to Joseph, 'I want you to go and
find your brothers. Take them some
food and see if they are well.'

Joseph walked and walked. His brothers saw him coming. They laughed behind their hands.

'Here comes the Great Dreamer,' they said.

One of them said, 'I've had enough of his dreams. He's only come now so that he can go back and tell our father about us. Let's kill him.'

Another one said, 'Why don't we just throw him in that well over there?'

They all thought that was the best idea. They took off Joseph's special coat and threw him into the dried-up well.

Then they sat down to enjoy the food
Joseph had brought them.

Suddenly they saw a long line of
camels walking slowly over the hills.
They knew the men with the camels
were going to Egypt to sell their goods.

'I know,' one brother said. 'Let's sell
Joseph to those men. They can take him
to Egypt to work. Then we'll never see
him again.'

They shouted to the men to stop. Then they pulled Joseph up out of the well.

'What will you pay us for this strong young man?' they asked.

Joseph's brothers sold him to the men for twenty silver coins and watched the camels go off to Egypt with Joseph walking behind.

They tore Joseph's coat and dipped it in the blood of an animal. The beautiful new coat looked horrible now.

When they went home they tried to
look unhappy.

'Look what we've found,' they said to
Jacob, holding up the coat. 'Do you
think Joseph has been killed by a wild
animal?'

Jacob took the coat and held it up.
'Joseph must be dead,' he said.
　　Jacob was so sad. He did not see that
his sons were glad to get rid of Joseph.

The brothers did not know that God
had important work for Joseph to do in
Egypt.

But first there were things Joseph
must learn.

Jacob was very sad. He thought that he would never see Joseph again. He did not know then that this was not the end of the story.

The Lion Story Bible is made up of 52 individual stories for young readers, building up an understanding of the Bible as one story – God's story – a story for all time and all people.

The Old Testament section (numbers 1-30) tells the story of a great nation – God's chosen people, the Israelites – and God's love and care for them through good times and bad. The stories are about people who knew and trusted God. From this nation came one special person, Jesus Christ, sent by God to save all people everywhere.

The story of *Joseph the dreamer* comes from the first book of the Bible, Genesis chapter 37. Joseph, the youngest but one of Jacob's twelve sons (who gave their names to the twelve tribes of Israel), is one of the outstanding characters of the Old Testament. Like many of the Bible's heroes he was far from perfect, but God used him none the less to forward his great, unfolding plan of salvation.

The next story in the series, number 8: *Joseph and the king of Egypt,* tells how Joseph rose from slavery to being governor of all Egypt, and how he saved his family in a time of famine.